The Bridge

The Bridge

Shauntay Grant

Playwrights Canada Press
Toronto

LIBRARY AND ARCHIVES CANADA CATALOGUING IN PUBLICATION
Title: The bridge / Shauntay Grant.
Names: Grant, Shauntay, author.
Description: A play.
Identifiers: Canadiana (print) 20210139390 | Canadiana (ebook) 20210139420 | ISBN 9780369102263 (softcover) | ISBN 9780369102270 (PDF) | ISBN 9780369102287 (HTML) | ISBN 9780369102294 (Kindle)
Classification: LCC PS8613.R3663 B75 2021 | DDC C812/.6—dc23

Playwrights Canada Press operates on Mississaugas of the Credit, Wendat, Anishinaabe, Métis, and Haudenosaunee land. It always was and always will be Indigenous land.

We acknowledge the financial support of the Canada Council for the Arts, the Ontario Arts Council (OAC), Ontario Creates, and the Government of Canada for our publishing activities.

Playwright's Note

About fifteen years ago I woke up one morning and began the unfamiliar task of piecing together a handful of old poems—verses that had no bearing on one another, yet in those early hours something compelled me to look for patterns, connection, parallel themes, a bridge among them. I took up each individual text and treated it as an unrefined, deliberate piece of a large puzzle. I cut them up and laid the language down, shuffling metaphors like cards across my kitchen table. Extracting narratives—some for storing, some for keeping. And what was kept I carefully considered, polished, and pieced together as the bones of what I thought could be a play.

This is how I first learned to be a playwright. Not by rote or reading or writing workshops—that came later. My first meaningful encounter with this craft I've come to love was through poetry. And I realize now, in all my writing (be it poetry, plays, picture books . . .), I tend to approach language as a poet concerned with voice and cadence, metaphor and symbolism, and—in works like *The Bridge*—making space for conversation between the natural and the supernatural world. A bridge of sorts: one that questions the polarity and pairing of the sacred and the secular in religion, in music, in people.

There have been many inspirations for this play along the way, but I must acknowledge its earliest influences: the Song of Solomon (King James Version), and the incomparable delta blues singer and guitarist Eddie James "Son" House Jr., whose 1965 recording of "John the Revelator" quite frankly woke me up. I'd also be remiss if I didn't acknowledge my Black Nova Scotian upbringing—the language and culture and community that helped shape me, and the traditional gospel music that has been somewhat of an enduring soundtrack from the womb.

Finally, a heartfelt thanks to everyone who helped make this play possible—my family and friends, colleagues and collaborators, sponsors and supporters, mentors and muses . . . to each of you, my gratitude and love.

Shauntay Grant
Halifax, Nova Scotia

The Bridge was first produced by 2b theatre company and Neptune Theatre in association with Obsidian Theatre Company at Neptune Theatre's Fountain Hall, Halifax, from January 22 to February 10, 2019, with the following cast and creative team:

John Solomon Moses: Jacob Sampson
Anna Moses/Ghost Anna: Sophia Walker
Samuel Moses: Daniel Ellis
Revered Eli: Jim Codrington
Chorister 1: Murleta Williams
Chorister 2: Charla Williams
Chorister 3: Chiamaka G. Ugwu

Director: Anthony Black
Assistant Director: Luciana Fernandes
Production and Stage Manager: Sylvia Bell
Assistant Stage Manager: Olivia McGinn
Set, Prop, and Costume Design: Rachel Forbes
Assistant Set, Prop, and Costume Design: Katrin Whitehead
Lighting Design: Leigh Ann Vardy
Assistant Lighting Design: Chelsey Jenkins
Script Supervisor / 2b Student Rep: Rooks Field-Green

Characters

John Solomon Moses: Fifty-five years old in 2010. Woodcarver. Self-taught musician. Haunted by his dead wife's ghost.

Ghost Anna Moses:* Ghost of John Solomon's dead wife. Thirty years old. Nine months pregnant. Appears only in 2010.

Young Anna Moses:* John Solomon's wife. Thirty years old. Appears only in 1988.

Samuel Moses: John Solomon's son. Twenty-two years old in 2010. Fourth-year university music major.

Reverend Eli: John Solomon's brother. Fifty-two years old in 2010. Baptist minister. Samuel's biological father.

Chorister 1: Adult female. Fifty plus years old. Appears only in 2010.

Chorister 2: Adult female. Fifty plus years old. Appears only in 2010.

Chorister 3: Adult female. Fifty plus years old. Appears only in 2010.

---

* Ghost Anna and Young Anna are played by the same actor. Although deceased, Ghost Anna is very much "alive" in the scenes. She is most active when she is in the house with John. She has more presence when Samuel or Eli are near John. No one can hear the ghost, but John can feel her presence and can sometimes almost hear her words. The ghost will at times shift things inside the house as a way of reaching out to John. If the ghost is in a very emotional state she may move objects (e.g., opening a Bible).

All characters serve as part of a singing ensemble when not delivering lines, contributing to the musical soundscape that permeates the play.

Setting

Set in a rural Black community in Nova Scotia, a crooked bridge acts as a gateway between "heaven" (church, burial grounds) and "earth" (John Solomon's home).

The kitchen is simple—table, chairs, wood stove. There are two entrances to the living room—the front door and a hallway entrance.

The church is an intimate, modestly decorated sanctuary with wooden pews and a wooden pulpit. The pulpit is raised.

Time

The play moves between 1988 and late spring of 2010.

Text

Text in "quotations" indicates biblical text. The language in the community is rooted in Black Nova Scotian vernacular and carries a certain quickness—this shows especially when emotions are high (excitement, anger, frustration . . .) or when conversation is fuelled by gossip (e.g., the choristers' gossip). Moments of overlapping dialogue are sometimes marked by a forward slash (/).

Act 1
Scene 1

The year is 2010. The CHORISTERS *whisper inaudible gossip from off stage.* REVEREND ELI *is at church.* JOHN SOLOMON *is at home.*

CHORISTER 1
(singing from off stage) There is a balm in Gilead
To make the wounded whole

JOHN SOLOMON whittles a wooden cross. GHOST ANNA places a Bible on the table.

There is a balm in Gilead
To heal the sin-sick soul

GHOST ANNA retrieves YOUNG ANNA's shawl. JOHN SOLOMON notices the Bible.

Sometimes I feel discouraged
And think my work's in vain

GHOST ANNA drapes YOUNG ANNA's shawl across an empty chair as JOHN SOLOMON puts the Bible back in its hiding place.

But then the holy spirit
Revives my soul again

JOHN SOLOMON sees the shawl and puts it back in its hiding place. GHOST ANNA hangs a portrait of YOUNG ANNA on the wall.

Revives my soul again

JOHN SOLOMON sees the portrait and removes it from the wall.

CHORISTERS
(singing) There is a balm in Gilead
To make the wounded whole

JOHN SOLOMON puts the portrait in a hiding place. SAMUEL arrives home with luggage.

There is a balm in Gilead
To heal the sin-sick soul

JOHN SOLOMON sits whittling a wooden cross.

Scene 2

GHOST ANNA
"Let not your heart be troubled.

JOHN SOLOMON reacts.

"Ye believe in God, believe also in me."

Beat.

"In my Father's house are many mansions: if it were not so, I would have told you."

SAMUEL
Pops.

GHOST ANNA recites scripture against SAMUEL and JOHN SOLOMON's dialogue.

GHOST ANNA	**SAMUEL**
"I go to prepare a place for you. And if I go and prepare a place for you, I will come again, and receive you unto myself that where I am, there ye may be also."	Pops.
Beat.	*Beat.*
"Jesus saith unto him, I am the way, the truth, and the life: no man cometh unto the Father, but by me."	So, what? We just not goin'?
Beat.	*Beat.*
"If ye had known me, ye should have known my Father also: and from henceforth ye know Him! and have seen Him!"	Pops.

JOHN SOLOMON
Sammy!

Beat.

When you ever know me to go up to church?

SAMUEL
I can't believe this. Your own mother's funeral.

JOHN SOLOMON
And the devil bringin' the word.

SAMUEL
He's your brother.

JOHN SOLOMON
The devil.

SAMUEL
He's the reverend, for God sakes.

JOHN SOLOMON
The hell he is. Any fool can preach a sermon.

GHOST ANNA
(singing) If you can't preach like Peter . . .

GHOST ANNA sings "There Is a Balm in Gilead" through the scene.

SAMUEL
Well that "fool" is the only one doin' right by Mama right now.

JOHN SOLOMON
Doin right / by . . . ?

SAMUEL
Mama Irenie ain't had but two sons.

JOHN SOLOMON
And what you know about it?

SAMUEL
What you think people gonna say if he the only one showin' up for the family?

JOHN SOLOMON
Family?

SAMUEL
"So what" you ain't been to church in forever.

JOHN SOLOMON
You wanna preach to ***me*** / about family?

SAMUEL
Your mother just *died*, Pops!

JOHN SOLOMON
Four years you been gone, up Toronto payin' five thousand dollas a year for some damn singin' lessons . . .

SAMUEL
Here we go.

JOHN SOLOMON
. . . when you coulda stayed home, went to / school.

SAMUEL
I'm a music major.

JOHN SOLOMON
And they don't got music major down home?

SAMUEL
We already been through this.

JOHN SOLOMON
Four years, Sammy. And you gonna come home preach to me / about family?

The argument intensifies, overlapping each other.

SAMUEL
I'm just sayin'. Go to your mother's funeral. If ever there was a time to make an exception . . . just this once you think you'd find it in your heart to just . . . Just put family first, for Mama's sake. I can't believe you not even tryin' to go!

JOHN SOLOMON
Where were you when I was takin' care of Mama? Every minute out the road gettin' her groceries and her pills, takin' a hammer to the roof when it start leakin' and the plumbin' went, wipin' Mama *shit* stains off the floor—don't you *dare* talk to me 'bout family!

GHOST ANNA's singing intensifies.

SAMUEL
Right. 'Cause what I know 'bout family? I got a uncle I can't even talk to—let alone look at—and I don't even know why.

JOHN SOLOMON
'Cause he's the devil!

SAMUEL
A grandmother I can't bury 'cause I'm a grown-ass man who ain't allowed / up church.

JOHN SOLOMON
A grown-ass man who need to shut the hell up and stop talkin' back.

SAMUEL
And a dead mother I know almost nothin' about except the couple stories I got from Mama Irenie, but *you*? You won't so much as even tell me what she like to eat for breakfast in the mornin'.

JOHN SOLOMON
(threateningly) Sammy . . . That's enough. I said that's enough!

(to GHOST ANNA*)* Anna!

SAMUEL reacts; GHOST ANNA stops singing abruptly. Beat.

SAMUEL
Pops?

JOHN SOLOMON sits whittling a wooden cross.

Can we at least go to the burial?

Beat.

Pops.

JOHN SOLOMON
Sammy.

Beat.

G'on then. G'on if you wanna go.

JOHN SOLOMON whittles a wooden cross. The CHORISTERS whisper. SAMUEL retrieves his luggage and exits to the back room. GHOST ANNA retrieves the family Bible and arranges it on the table; JOHN SOLOMON reacts and cuts himself with the carving knife.

Ah! Dammit!

Scene 3

In 1988 JOHN SOLOMON sucks blood from his wound.

YOUNG ANNA
Let me see it.

YOUNG ANNA sits facing JOHN SOLOMON, their knees touching. CHORISTER 3 hums "Jesus Loves Me."

JOHN SOLOMON
It's fine.

YOUNG ANNA
John.

JOHN SOLOMON
I said it's fine.

YOUNG ANNA removes the shawl from around her shoulders and drapes it over both of their legs. She dumps first aid supplies on the shawl and persuades JOHN SOLOMON to let her look at his wounded hand.

YOUNG ANNA
Fine like the time y'almost cut y'arm off out on the woodpile?

JOHN SOLOMON
Come on now.

YOUNG ANNA
Or is it fine like that time you come home wit' a wood chip the size of this finger jammed in ya butt cheeks.

YOUNG ANNA motions with her finger.

JOHN SOLOMON
I told Eli he need to get someone come sand down them rickety old church pews. Board so rough it'd scrape ya butts off too.

YOUNG ANNA
Mmmm. G'on. Blame it on the reverend.

YOUNG ANNA
Or are you just "fine" like the time you went out and amputated ya foot off / messin' 'round wit' my cookin' knife.

JOHN SOLOMON
It was my baby toe.

YOUNG ANNA
Got you half limpin'.

JOHN SOLOMON
Still walkin', ain't I?

YOUNG ANNA applies alcohol to JOHN SOLOMON's wound with a cotton swab. JOHN SOLOMON reacts.

YOUNG ANNA
(laughing) Worse than a two-year-old.

YOUNG ANNA dresses JOHN SOLOMON's wound with a bandage.

You know this woulda never happened / if you had just . . .

JOHN SOLOMON
Now here you go.

YOUNG ANNA
I'm just sayin'.

JOHN SOLOMON
Anna.

Beat.

YOUNG ANNA
There.

YOUNG ANNA is done dressing JOHN SOLOMON's wound. She caresses/kisses his bandaged hand. JOHN SOLOMON pulls away and retreats to the back room.

Scene 4

CHORISTER 3 is still humming. YOUNG ANNA sits alone reading her Bible. REVEREND ELI is at the church pulpit.

REVEREND ELI & YOUNG ANNA
(reading) "The song of songs, which is Solomon's."

Beat.

"Let him kiss me with the kisses of his mouth; For love is better than wine."

JOHN SOLOMON reacts, enters from the back room.

YOUNG ANNA speaks to JOHN SOLOMON.

"Because of the savour of thy good ointments, thy name is as ointment poured forth."

JOHN SOLOMON reacts.

YOUNG ANNA
(to JOHN SOLOMON) "Draw me."

REVEREND ELI reacts, sees YOUNG ANNA. JOHN SOLOMON leaves.

(calling after JOHN SOLOMON) "Draw me."

Beat.

"I am black, but comely. Comely as the tents of Kedar, comely as the curtains of Solomon, I am . . . "

"Jesus Loves Me" transitions into a funeral wail sung by the ENSEMBLE.

REVEREND ELI
"Comely. Thou art comely."

Beat.

"Thou art comely as the tents of Kedar, comely as Jerusalem, and thy love is better than wine."

YOUNG ANNA and REVEREND ELI meet on the bridge.

YOUNG ANNA
"My mother's children were angry with me. They made me the keeper of the vineyards; but mine own vineyard have I not kept."

REVEREND ELI
"Thy love is better than wine."

YOUNG ANNA
(to God) "Tell me, O thou whom my soul loveth, where thou feedest, where thou makes thy flock to rest at noon. For why should I be as one turned aside by the flocks of thy companions?"

(to REVEREND ELI) "I have compared thee, O my love, to a company of horses in Pharaoh's chariots."

REVEREND ELI
"Thy cheeks are comely with rows of jewels, thy neck with chains of gold."

YOUNG ANNA
"Mine own vineyard have I / not . . . "

REVEREND ELI
"We will make thee borders of gold with studs of silver."

YOUNG ANNA
"I have / not . . . "

REVEREND ELI
"While the king sitteth at his table, my spikenard sendeth forth the smell thereof."

YOUNG ANNA
"A bundle of myrrh is my well-beloved unto me. He shall lie all night betwixt my breasts . . . "

REVEREND ELI
"Shhh."

REVEREND ELI kisses YOUNG ANNA on the neck.

YOUNG ANNA
(resisting) "Behold."

The ENSEMBLE stops humming. YOUNG ANNA opens her blouse and indicates her chest, a scar where her breast once was.

"Behold."

REVEREND ELI
(interrupting) "Behold, thou art fair . . . my love."

JOHN SOLOMON starts toe-tapping.

"Behold, thou art fair; Thou hast doves' eyes."

REVEREND ELI and YOUNG ANNA kiss.

JOHN SOLOMON
(singing) Tell me who's that writin'? John the Revelator
Who's that writin'? John the Revelator
Well who's that writin'? John the Revelator
Wrote the book of the seven seals

You know God walked down in the cool of the day
Called Adam by his name
And he refused to answer
Because he naked and ashamed

Scene 5

In 2010 JOHN SOLOMON *is at home singing/toe-tapping and whittling a wooden cross.*

JOHN SOLOMON
(singing) Tell me who's that writin'? John the Revelator
Who's that writin'? John the Revelator
Well who's that writin'? John the Revelator
Wrote the book . . .

SAMUEL *enters; he is dressed for Mama Irenie's funeral.* JOHN SOLOMON *sees* SAMUEL *and stops singing abruptly.* SAMUEL *exits through the front door—he pauses on the front porch, then moves to go back inside, but stops before opening the door.*

SAMUEL *sings—gently, but loud enough so that* JOHN SOLOMON *can hear him.*

SAMUEL
I'm gonna meet my mother in the wilderness

JOHN SOLOMON *reacts.*

The wilderness, the wilderness

SAMUEL *hears movement from* JOHN SOLOMON.

I'm gonna meet my mother in the wilderness
One of those days

SAMUEL listens for more movement from JOHN SOLOMON. Hearing nothing, he leaves for the funeral, humming the chorus of the song. GHOST ANNA places the Bible on the table. JOHN SOLOMON ignores her and continues whittling his cross in silence.

Scene 6

The ENSEMBLE sings the chorus of "In the Sweet By and By" as the scene transitions.

ENSEMBLE
(singing) In the sweet by and by
We shall meet on that beautiful shore
In the sweet by and by
We shall meet on that beautiful shore

The ENSEMBLE continues to hum "In the Sweet By and By." At church, REVEREND ELI preaches at Mama Irenie's funeral service; the CHORISTERS interject with quick banter.

REVEREND ELI
There is a bridge between heaven and earth.

CHORISTER 1
Reverend got one foot in the world and one foot in the church.

REVEREND ELI
And no one knows the way except God.

SAMUEL enters the church.

CHORISTER 1
Well Lawd . . .

CHORISTER 3
That ain't Sammy?

CHORISTER 2
Sure is.

CHORISTER 3
My Lord.

CHORISTER 1
I can't believe John Solomon 'llowed him up church!

REVEREND ELI sees SAMUEL.

REVEREND ELI
God the everlasting Father. The Alpha and Omega. The beginning and the end. The first and the last.

CHORISTER 2
You think John Solomon woulda come—was his own mother passed.

CHORISTER 1
Well he didn't bury his wife.

CHORISTER 3
You said it.

REVEREND ELI
When the last trumpet sound and the final day has passed . . .

CHORISTER 1
Didn't the reverend preach this sermon at the last funeral?

REVEREND ELI
. . . the revelation of Jesus Christ shall show His face anew to that blessed soul who kept His word and lived a life that's true.

CHORISTER 1
The *same sermon* he preached for Grandfather Kennie.

CHORISTER 2
I know.

CHORISTER 3
(to CHORISTERS 1 & 2) Shhh!

REVEREND ELI
He whose voice is like the sound / of many waters flow.

CHORISTER 1
And Aunt Paulina.

REVEREND ELI
He who purged / the sinner's soul and washed you pure as snow.

CHORISTER 2
Brother Bobbie.

CHORISTER 1
Don't forget Cousin Doug.

CHORISTER 3
(to REVEREND ELI) Amen, Reverend!

REVEREND ELI
He who has the power / to remove each and every stain.

CHORISTER 2
My Lord.

CHORISTER 1
The *same / sermon*.

CHORISTER 3
(to REVEREND ELI) Amen, amen, amen!

REVEREND ELI
He who takes the empty cup and make you whole again.

CHORISTER 2
A sin and shame.

REVEREND ELI
Come on now, church. Sing.

The CHORISTERS start singing immediately and enthusiastically.

CHORISTERS
(singing) I met my dear old mother
She was climbin' up the hill so slow
She was tryin' to get to heaven in due time
Before the heaven door close

Before the heaven door close
Before the heaven door close
She was tryin' to get to heaven in due time
Before the heaven door close

The CHORISTERS *stop singing abruptly.* REVEREND ELI *stands alone at Mama Irenie's gravesite.*

REVEREND ELI
Mama, you have been . . .

The CHORISTERS *hum "I'm Gonna Meet My Mother in the Wilderness."*

(to God) Take your rest, dear Mama.
Come down from glory, blessed redeemer.

YOUNG ANNA *is revealed in 1988. She prays.*

YOUNG ANNA
"Have mercy on me, O God."

REVEREND ELI	**YOUNG ANNA**
You are the Alpha and Omega. You are the beginning and the end. You are that which was and is to come. We commit Your faithful and humble servant to you. Dear Lord, come. Holy Spirit, come.	According to thy loving kindness. According unto the multitude of thy tender mercies. Blot out my transgressions. Cleanse me from my sin.

YOUNG ANNA
"Cleanse me from my sin."

REVEREND ELI
Come.

YOUNG ANNA
"Cleanse me from my / sin."

REVEREND ELI
(to YOUNG ANNA) Come. Anna.

Scene 7

It is 1988. YOUNG ANNA moves between two separate scenes—one with REVEREND ELI, the other with JOHN SOLOMON.

REVEREND ELI
We need to talk.

YOUNG ANNA
What we need to do is pray.

REVEREND ELI
Then come, let's pray.

YOUNG ANNA
I been prayin'!

REVEREND ELI
I know.

YOUNG ANNA
What you know? You know what it like to get sick? To have your breast cut off? To have your husband scared to look at you like a woman?

REVEREND ELI
Anna.

YOUNG ANNA
I betrayed my marriage!

REVEREND ELI & JOHN SOLOMON
Anna, listen.

YOUNG ANNA
(to JOHN) No you listen!

JOHN SOLOMON
What more you want, Anna?

YOUNG ANNA
How 'bout I want my husband back!

JOHN SOLOMON
I'm right / here.

YOUNG ANNA
How 'bout that.

JOHN SOLOMON
Anna, I been here.

YOUNG ANNA
You ain't been here since the operation.

JOHN SOLOMON
Who the one drove you back and forth / to the doctor's and and and . . .

YOUNG ANNA
A dog coulda drove me back and forth to the doctor's, John.

JOHN SOLOMON
. . . who the one stayed with you through the surgery and brung you home and cared for you / all that time when you was . . .

YOUNG ANNA
You put me off on Mama Irenie and locked yourself in the back room for four days.

JOHN SOLOMON
I needed my space.

YOUNG ANNA
And I needed my husband.

Beat.

JOHN SOLOMON
(tenderly) Anna.

JOHN SOLOMON embraces YOUNG ANNA from behind—it's the first time he's embraced her since her surgery. YOUNG ANNA turns to face her husband. YOUNG ANNA unbuttons JOHN SOLOMON's shirt. JOHN SOLOMON resists.

YOUNG ANNA
John.

JOHN SOLOMON
I can't—I . . . Anna, I'm sorry I . . . I can't.

Beat.

REVEREND ELI
Anna.

YOUNG ANNA crosses to REVEREND ELI.

YOUNG ANNA
When you and I . . .

Beat.

John and I were . . .

Beat.

I didn't mean for us / to . . .

REVEREND ELI
Anna.

Beat.

You and me. We go way back.

Beat.

You must have felt something / when we . . .

YOUNG ANNA
Eli, I love him.

Beat.

What we did was wrong.

REVEREND ELI
Anna, I . . .

YOUNG ANNA
(to JOHN) I'm pregnant.

REVEREND ELI
What?

JOHN SOLOMON
But that ain't possible.

Beat.

YOUNG ANNA
I'm so sorry I . . .

JOHN SOLOMON
We ain't been . . .

Beat.

YOUNG ANNA
John.

Beat.

It only happened one time, / I swear to God I . . .

JOHN SOLOMON
Oh, Anna.

YOUNG ANNA
If I could I'd take it back, you know I would, John. I / love you and I . . .

JOHN SOLOMON
Anna, how could you.

YOUNG ANNA
I don't know I don't know I don't know I / was just . . .

JOHN SOLOMON
How could you!

YOUNG ANNA
John, I'm so sorry. I love you / so much and I . . .

JOHN SOLOMON
Stop it. Stop it.

YOUNG ANNA
Please, John! I'll do anything to make it right I . . .

JOHN SOLOMON exits.

John.

REVEREND ELI
Anna.

Beat.

Anna, if John ever found out / that we . . .

YOUNG ANNA
He knows.

REVEREND ELI
What?

YOUNG ANNA
He knows.

REVEREND ELI
Does he know that I'm / the . . .

YOUNG ANNA
Who else would it be?

REVEREND ELI
Oh, Anna. Why?

YOUNG ANNA
Well what else could I do?

REVEREND ELI
But why'd you have to / tell him?

YOUNG ANNA
We ain't been together in months so he was gonna find out somehow.

REVEREND ELI
But we coulda dealt with this some other way.

YOUNG ANNA
Eli, that ain't Christian. And you of all people / should know . . .

REVEREND ELI
I didn't mean *that*!

YOUNG ANNA
Well how else was you gonna deal with it?

REVEREND ELI
I don't know but there had to be some other way. / Do you have any idea what . . .

YOUNG ANNA
Wasn't no other way 'bout it. I had to tell him.

REVEREND ELI
What were you thinking, Anna?

YOUNG ANNA
And I thought if he knew how sorry I was eventually he'd / forgive me but . . .

REVEREND ELI
This ain't happenin'.

YOUNG ANNA
. . . it's been weeks now and he won't / even . . .

REVEREND ELI
It ain't happenin'.

YOUNG ANNA
. . . he won't even talk to . . .

JOHN SOLOMON is heard tuning his guitar.

YOUNG ANNA & REVEREND ELI
(simultaneously) Oh God.

YOUNG ANNA approaches JOHN SOLOMON.

YOUNG ANNA
John.

JOHN SOLOMON is unresponsive, continues tuning his guitar.

REVEREND ELI
John.

JOHN SOLOMON stops tuning his guitar.

Brother.

JOHN SOLOMON reacts.

Brother, we need to talk.

JOHN SOLOMON attacks REVEREND ELI.

Act 2

Scene 1

The ENSEMBLE *picks up the funeral wail. In 2010* SAMUEL *is at* ANNA*'s gravesite. The* CHORISTERS *gossip.*

CHORISTER 1
Remember how the reverend got Sister Anna pregnant?

CHORISTER 2
You believe that?

CHORISTER 3
I thought that boy was John's baby?

CHORISTER 1
Someone said he was the reverend's.

CHORISTER 3
That ain't true.

CHORISTER 2
You never know. Anna *was* courtin' two brothers.

CHORISTER 3
But she and the reverend was a old-school thing. Long before he went into the ministry. Him and Anna was broke up *years* before her and John—she was married!

CHORISTER 2
Dirt digglin' with the reverend she was.

CHORISTER 1 reacts.

CHORISTER 3
Sister Anna wasn't like that.

CHORISTER 1
Well the reverend sure was.

CHORISTER 2
Was?

CHORISTERS 1 & 2 slap five.

CHORISTER 3
Just 'cause he look good don't make him a runaround.

CHORISTER 2
Hmph.

CHORISTER 3
He's our pastor!

CHORISTER 1
He looks good.

CHORISTER 2
He ain't all that.

CHORISTER 1
Who ain't?

CHORISTER 3
Stop that.

CHORISTER 1
That man could tempt the bloomers off the Virgin Mary if he wanted to.

CHORISTER 2
So then who's to say him and Anna . . .

CHORISTER 1
That's what I'm tryin' to tell / ya.

CHORISTER 3
You fell's is so nas-ty.

CHORISTERS 1 & 2
I'm just sayin'.

CHORISTER 2
Remember now that John wasn't speakin' to the reverend 'fore Anna died.

CHORISTERS 1 & 3
(nodding in agreement) Mmm hmm.

CHORISTER 2
And he didn't come to Anna's funeral neither.*

CHORISTER 1
Well the reverend preached the sermon.

---

* Pronounced "nee-ther."

CHORISTER 2
Plus the baby come too quick. Right the same time she died. Poor Sammy probably killed his own mama.

CHORISTER 3
You believe that?

CHORISTER 2
Well . . .

CHORISTER 1
I heard John Solomon and the reverend had it out somethin' *terrible*!

CHORISTERS 2 & 3
No!

CHORISTER 1
John Solomon knocked the reverend out *good*!

CHORISTER 2
What!?

CHORISTER 3
And he wasn't even speakin' to Anna 'fore she died, you know.

CHORISTER 2
For real?

CHORISTER 3
That what I heard.

CHORISTER 2
That g'on' come back to haunt him.

The funeral wail stops. JOHN SOLOMON and GHOST ANNA are at home. GHOST ANNA is moving about the house, muttering scripture and trying to get JOHN SOLOMON's attention by retrieving the shawl, Bible, and portrait from their hiding places and arranging them around the room, one at a time; JOHN SOLOMON counters by putting everything back in its hiding place.

CHORISTER 3
You said it.

The CHORISTERS/funeral wail resume.

CHORISTER 2
Lord. If John Solomon was any kinda Christian / he . . .

CHORISTER 1
If the reverend was any kinda Christian . . .

CHORISTER 3
Stop that!

CHORISTER 1
I'm just sayin'.

CHORISTER 3
He's our / pastor!

CHORISTERS 1 & 2
(to CHORISTER 3) Shhh!

The ENSEMBLE stops humming abruptly. CHORISTER 1 motions towards REVEREND ELI, who is approaching SAMUEL at ANNA's gravesite. The CHORISTERS look on.

Scene 2

JOHN SOLOMON hums "There Is a Balm in Gilead." In 2010 SAMUEL stands alone at his mother's gravesite. REVEREND ELI approaches.

REVEREND ELI
Take your time, son.

SAMUEL
Thank you, Reverend.

JOHN SOLOMON stops humming.

REVEREND ELI
You can call me "uncle" you know.

JOHN SOLOMON
Samuel Jeremiah Ezekial Leviticus Moses!

JOHN SOLOMON is at home in 1996. SAMUEL speaks to him as his eight-year-old self. CHORISTER 3 hums "Jesus Loves Me."

SAMUEL
Pops!

JOHN SOLOMON
Where you at, boy?

SAMUEL
Here, I'm . . . I'm comin', Pops!

JOHN SOLOMON
Well hurry up, it's past your bedtime. You finish your homework?

SAMUEL
Yessir.

JOHN SOLOMON
Do your chores?

SAMUEL
Yessir.

JOHN SOLOMON
Brush your teeth. Say your prayers.

SAMUEL
Yessir.

JOHN SOLOMON
Good, now listen. Rocky just called say he seen you up by the church after school today.

SAMUEL
I was / just . . .

JOHN SOLOMON
What I tell you 'bout goin' up 'round there?

SAMUEL
But I wasn't doin' / nothin'.

JOHN SOLOMON
"But I wasn't" nothin'.

SAMUEL
But it's Tuesday and the reverend wasn't / even up there today.

JOHN SOLOMON
Boy, what I tell you 'bout talkin' back?

SAMUEL
I only just went to the graveyard to see Mum.

JOHN SOLOMON
I already done told you. Now I don't wanna hear 'bout you goin' up 'round the church Tuesday, Wednesday, Thursday, or any other day. That man is the devil. And you is a child a God. From now on after school no playin' around—you come straight home, you hear me?

SAMUEL
Yessir.

JOHN SOLOMON
And if I ever hear tell 'bout you runnin' up church again you gon' get it, y'understand?

SAMUEL
Yessir.

JOHN SOLOMON
What you say?

SAMUEL
Yessir.

Beat.

JOHN SOLOMON
Aight then. Now c'mon. G'on. Get in bed.

(gently) Get you in tight under the covers. Don't want you catch cold now. You warm enough?

SAMUEL
Yessir.

JOHN SOLOMON
You sure now? I got another blanket warmin' out by the stove if you want.

SAMUEL
I'm okay.

JOHN SOLOMON
Aight then. You go right to sleep now.

CHORISTER 3 stops humming.

SAMUEL
Can you sing me a song?

JOHN SOLOMON
What?

SAMUEL
That song you was just singin'. Can you teach it to me? You know . . .

SAMUEL starts humming "There Is a Balm in Gilead."

JOHN SOLOMON
After all that practisin' we did today? Ain't you sung enough for one night?

SAMUEL
Nope.

JOHN SOLOMON
(laughing) Boy, you sumthin' else.

SAMUEL
Please, Pops? I promise I'll go right to sleep after.

JOHN SOLOMON
The hell you will. I know your tricks.

SAMUEL
I mean it!

JOHN SOLOMON
Not tonight. It's late and you got school in the mornin'.

SAMUEL
Tomorrow?

JOHN SOLOMON
Maybe tomorrow. Aight then?

SAMUEL
Aight then.

Beat.

JOHN SOLOMON
G'night, Sammy.

SAMUEL
G'night, Pops.

SAMUEL hums "There Is a Balm in Gilead" as he crosses to REVEREND ELI; JOHN SOLOMON listens.

REVEREND ELI
(to SAMUEL) You should come see me sometime.

Beat.

I have a necklace that belonged to your mother—a prayer cross. I've been trying to get it to you but John . . .

Beat.

I'm sure Anna would want you to have it. Why don't you stop by the church later on and I'll fetch it for you.

Beat.

Okay then. Take your time, son.

REVEREND ELI exits; SAMUEL stands alone at his mother's gravesite.

SAMUEL
Mum.

Scene 3

In 2010 the CHORISTERS *move through the church burial grounds. The* ENSEMBLE *hums "Before the Heaven Doors Close."*

CHORISTERS
(reading tombstone) Lord have mercy!

CHORISTER 3
Marcus Jeremiah Ross?

CHORISTER 2
I still can't believe they let you be buried 'longside the church.

CHORISTER 1
All that sinnin' you done did?

CHORISTERS
Lord!

CHORISTER 2
Break and enterin'.

CHORISTER 3
Armed robbery.

CHORISTER 1
Assault wit' a deadly weapon.

CHORISTER 3
Child abuse.

CHORISTER 2
Wife abuse.

CHORISTER 3
Fraud.

CHORISTERS
Ain't no *way* that man made it in.

CHORISTER 1
He mighta crossed the bridge. Made it far as heaven door. Might even got to knock knock knockin' on it but so help me, I tell you . . .

CHORISTER 2
(interrupting) Preach!

CHORISTER 1
. . . soon that angel Gabriel seen his sorry ass try to step through the pearly gates, I ***know*** he look Marcus Jeremiah straight in the eye and say, "You must be out ya goddamn mind!"

CHORISTER 3
(to CHORISTER 1) Stop that now.

CHORISTER 1
God rest his soul.

CHORISTER 2
Amen.

CHORISTER 1
Well will you look at that—someone went put fresh flowers on Brother Bobbie grave.

CHORISTER 2
Shoulda put a bucket of chicken. That man was sooo fat.

CHORISTERS 1 & 3 respond in agreement.

Took the whole community to lug his behind out the church when he passed. Casket so heavy Cousin Ronnie was pall-bearin' dropped his side, sent poor Aunt Paulina flyin' down the church steps, knocked that old woman straight out!

CHORISTER 1
Almost had two funerals in one day.

CHORISTER 2
That man been dead five years but believe you me there's enough meat on them bones to keep them maggots feastin' for forty, fifty years to come.

CHORISTER 3
God rest his soul.

CHORISTER 2
Amen.

CHORISTER 3
Well now will you look at that.

CHORISTERS pause at another gravesite.

Mary Elizabeth Carter.

CHORISTERS 1 & 2
My Lord.

CHORISTERS
I forgot you was even dead.

CHORISTER 1 spies JOHN SOLOMON standing at Mama Irenie's gravesite.

CHORISTER 3
Sorry I didn't make it out to your funeral.

CHORISTER 2
Me too. Heard it was a lovely time.

CHORISTER 1
(motioning towards JOHN SOLOMON) Look.

The humming stops. The CHORISTERS observe JOHN SOLOMON at Mama Irenie's gravesite.

CHORISTER 2
Irene Isabella Moses.

CHORISTER 1
(motioning to JOHN SOLOMON) Didn't even come to his own mama / funeral.

CHORISTER 3
Shhh!

CHORISTER 2
God rest your soul.

Lights fade on the CHORISTERS.

JOHN SOLOMON
(singing) I'm gonna meet my mother in the wilderness
The wilderness, the wilderness
I'm gonna meet my mother in the wilderness
One of those days

REVEREND ELI enters, spies his brother.

I'm goin' right straight up yonder
I'm goin' right straight up yonder
I'm goin' . . .

REVEREND ELI joins in.

JOHN SOLOMON & REVEREND ELI
(singing) . . . right straight . . .

JOHN SOLOMON stops singing.

REVEREND ELI
(singing) . . . up yonder
One of those days

JOHN SOLOMON exits abruptly.

(calling after JOHN SOLOMON) John!

REVEREND ELI moves to Mama Irenie's gravesite.

Scene 4

In 2010 REVEREND ELI stands alone at Mama Irenie's gravesite.

REVEREND ELI
Mama.

Beat.

It's Sunday, early evenin'. The wind has cooled down and the sun just beginnin' to scratch the big spruce on top of Mudder's Hill. Remember, Mama? The buttercups out in full bloom. The berries just ripe. Sour apples green and ropin'.

Beat.

In all my dreams, Samuel's gone almost two, three whole hours with his blue bucket and matchin' shovel—pickin' berries for Anna, and on the side just diggin' the earth for gold.

Beat.

He's just turned five.

Beat.

He starts school in September.

Beat.

You're in the kitchen, Mama, bakin' cornbread and singin' "Jesus Be a Fence" out loud and off-key. John and I are on the porch just . . . talkin' . . . sharin' scripture . . . waitin' for Samuel to come tearin' 'round the corner with a bucket fulla blueberries. He picked and picked so hard he almost missed the sun. But sure enough when the sky changed there he come runnin' . . . laughin' and screamin' "Daddy!"

Beat.

"Uncle Eli! Look what I got!"

Beat.

He runs up to the porch and plops the bucket on the first stoop, and he catches his breath while I go on and on about how that's the mostest berries I ever seen in one straight pickin'. He smiles. And he keeps on smilin' while John bends down and scoops him up high onto his shoulders. He reaches his little arms up and strokes the sky, back and forth as if it was a giant canvas and him alone paintin' the purple and rose that comes after the sun. And Anna . . .

Beat.

Anna is alive, and there with him. And we are all a family. And, Mama?

Beat.

Mama, I'm sorry.

Beat.

I'm so sorry.

The CHORISTERS *hum the "I'm Goin' Right Straight up Yonder" refrain from offstage.* REVEREND ELI *kneels to pray.*

Scene 5

In 2010 REVEREND ELI prays at Mama Irenie's gravesite. The CHORISTERS hum from offstage.

REVEREND ELI
"Have mercy upon me, O God, according to thy loving kindness: according unto the multitude of thy tender mercies blot out my transgressions."

JOHN SOLOMON is revealed on the bridge, drinking alcohol and reading/reciting scripture. The lights fade on REVEREND ELI as SAMUEL approaches JOHN SOLOMON.

REVEREND ELI & JOHN SOLOMON
"Wash me thoroughly from mine iniquity, and cleanse me from my sin. For I acknowledge my transgressions: and my sin is ever before me."

SAMUEL
What's with the Bible?

JOHN SOLOMON
Rocky gave it to me. Thought I was scared of it. Crazy bastard.

SAMUEL
But you ain't even a Christian.

Beat.

Are you?

JOHN SOLOMON
Hell no. I gave up on them hypocrites long time ago, whoopin' and hollerin', singin' and prayin' come Sunday, eatin' bread and sippin' grape drink thinkin' they done good, then g'on and step out the church sinnin' and fornicatin' like A PACK OF FRIGGEN MONKEYS!

He directs the last line towards the church.

Sin and gossip, pray to Jesus. Sin and gossip, pray to Jesus. I mean if Jesus came back right now see what been goin' on in his name, *trust* me! That brotha'd crucify himself all over again, burn this place up black as Sodom Gomorrah.

SAMUEL
Pops.

JOHN SOLOMON
Buncha heathens with no fuckin' respect.

SAMUEL
You're drinkin' gin and readin' the Bible.

JOHN SOLOMON
I like the psalms. Listen:

JOHN SOLOMON reads from the Bible in his best "preacher voice."

"By the rivers of Babylon."

The CHORISTERS hum the chorus of "Every Time I Feel the Spirit."

SAMUEL
I can't believe / this.

JOHN SOLOMON
"There we sat down, yea, we wept, when we remembered Zion."

SAMUEL
Pops.

JOHN SOLOMON
"We hanged our harps upon the willows in the midst thereof. For there they that carried us away captive required of us a song," you brilliant muh-fucka!

The CHORISTERS *stop singing abruptly.*

SAMUEL
Pops!

JOHN SOLOMON
I don't care what nobody say, that David was smokin' some good shit when he wrote that.

SAMUEL
God give me strength.

JOHN SOLOMON
Muh-fucka could write!

SAMUEL
I'mma pray for you, Pops.

JOHN SOLOMON
Don't waste your prayers on me, boy. I already done crossed my bridge. *And* made peace with the passage. I know where y'all think I'm goin', and to tell you the truth I don't give a shit. 'Cause all sin and fall short of the glory but the Bible says, "If we confess our sins He is faithful! and just! to forgive us! and to cleanse us from all unrighteousness."

He looks up to God

Forgive me, Lord, for I have sinned!

He takes a swig of alcohol.

(in jest) I'm sorry.

SAMUEL moves to leave. In 1988 REVEREND ELI stands at the church pulpit; he flips through a thick Bible.

(to SAMUEL) Can't take it, can you. But it's in the word. And the truth shall set you free!

SAMUEL
It doesn't work like that and you know it.

JOHN SOLOMON
Well how do it work then? God put us all here—right smack in the middle of the goddamn orchard fulla bright red delicious apples and what he say? "Don't eat shit." Don't bite the apple.

SAMUEL
He's just testing us.

JOHN SOLOMON
Test my ass.

SAMUEL
Listen, / Pops . . .

JOHN SOLOMON
Look!

JOHN SOLOMON pulls an apple from his pocket. YOUNG ANNA is revealed lying naked on a bed, her back facing the audience. REVEREND ELI reads from a Bible.

REVEREND ELI
"The song of songs, which is Solomon's."

JOHN SOLOMON
(offering apple to SAMUEL) Here.

REVEREND ELI
"Set me as a seal upon thine heart, as a seal upon thine arm . . . "

JOHN SOLOMON
(to SAMUEL) Red.

REVEREND ELI
"For love is strong as death."

JOHN SOLOMON
(to SAMUEL) Juicy.

REVEREND ELI
"Jealousy is cruel as the grave."

JOHN SOLOMON
(to SAMUEL) Don't bite it.

JOHN SOLOMON taunts SAMUEL with the apple.

(playfully) Don't. But here. But don't.

SAMUEL exits.

Scene 6

Still 1988; REVEREND ELI *is at church reading from the Bible.*

REVEREND ELI
"Many waters cannot quench love, neither can the floods drown it: if a man would give all the substance of his house for love, it would utterly be contemned."

REVEREND ELI *sees* YOUNG ANNA.

"We have a little sister, and she hath no breasts. What shall we do for our sister in the day when she shall be spoken for?"

The CHORISTERS *hum a funeral wail.*

YOUNG ANNA
"If she be a wall?"

REVEREND ELI
"We will build upon her a palace of silver."

YOUNG ANNA
"And if she be a door?"

REVEREND ELI *climbs into bed with* YOUNG ANNA.

REVEREND ELI
"If she be a door, we will enclose her with boards of cedar."

REVEREND ELI *is on top of* YOUNG ANNA; *she shifts to face him. In 2010* JOHN SOLOMON *is at home; he hums the chorus of "John the Revelator."*

YOUNG ANNA
(to REVEREND ELI) "I am a wall, and my breasts like towers: then was I in his eyes as one that found favour."

REVEREND ELI and YOUNG ANNA kiss/caress.

JOHN SOLOMON
(singing) You know God walked down in the cool of the day
Called Adam by his name
And he refused to answer
Because he naked and ashamed

Scene 7

JOHN SOLOMON hums "John the Revelator." In 2010 the CHORISTERS move through the church burial grounds—they pause at ANNA's gravesite.

CHORISTER 1
Anna Ingrid Moses.

CHORISTER 2
Tell it!

CHORISTER 3
Now hold on now.

CHORISTER 1
What can I say.

CHORISTER 2
Tell it!

CHORISTER 3
Loving wife.

CHORISTER 1
(to CHORISTER 2) She was lovin' all right.

CHORISTER 3
Devoted Christian.

CHORISTER 1
(to CHORISTER 2) Devoted as the day is long.

CHORISTER 3
Choir member.

CHORISTER 2
Fornicator.

CHORISTER 1 reacts.

CHORISTER 3
Sunday school teacher.

CHORISTER 1
Adulterator.

CHORISTER 2 reacts.

CHORISTER 1
All up and through the pulpit come Sunday, all twistin' and turnin' front the reverend smellin' of sex, makin' that man lose his damn mind.

CHORISTER 3
Quiet. Humble. Steadfast. A good-hearted, righteous, and *virtuous* woman if I ever seen one myself. Stop it! Stop it!

CHORISTER 3
You know she my cousin.

CHORISTER 1
(aside) Fruit don't fall too far / from the tree.

CHORISTER 3
What now?

CHORISTER 2
Come look over here.

Beat.

CHORISTER 3
Charles Richard Johnson.

CHORISTER 1 reacts.

CHORISTER 2
I can't even.

CHORISTER 1
Now what can be said about you.

CHORISTER 2
Two words.

CHORISTER 1
Antonia Smith.

CHORISTER 2
Angelina Morris.

CHORISTER 3
Lillian Brookes.

CHORISTER 2
Charla Brookes.

CHORISTER 1
Mabel Brookes.

CHORISTER 3
Chasity Brookes.

CHORISTER 2
Nasty.

CHORISTER 3
Man had *six* wives.

CHORISTER 1
Seven.

CHORISTER 2
Wives?

CHORISTERS 1 & 3
"Relations."

CHORISTER 2
They was related all right. Them Brookes girls was *first* cousins.

CHORISTER 3
Six of 'em. Lord.

CHORISTER 1
Seven I said.

CHORISTER 2
Courtin' 'em all at the same time.

CHORISTER 3
Seven?

CHORISTER 1 looks knowingly at CHORISTER 2.

CHORISTER 2
Seven who?

Beat.

CHORISTER 3
(to CHORISTER 2) Seven you?

CHORISTER 1 reacts.

CHORISTER 2
Now hold / on now.

CHORISTER 3
You was wit' cheatin' Charlie Johnson?

CHORISTER 2
(to CHORISTER 1) Who told you?

CHORISTER 1
You told me right now.

CHORISTER 2 reacts.

But I knew right when it happen. Night before that *one* time he / come to church.

CHORISTER 3
That time he come to church! I remember you come in all happy / and smilin' . . .

CHORISTER 1
Smilin' and smellin' of sex she was.

CHORISTER 2
I / never . . .

CHORISTER 3
Cheatin' Charlie Johnson.

CHORISTER 1
(laughing) Heh heh heh.

CHORISTER 1
(to CHORISTER 3) Believe it.

CHORISTER 3
And here I thought the man finally come up church to get his blessin's.

CHORISTER 1
She gave him his blessin's all right.

CHORISTER 2
I wasn't like that and you know it.

CHORISTER 1
(to CHORISTER 3, in jest) Praise the Lord.

CHORISTER 2
(motioning to another gravesite) Look over here.

CHORISTER 3
(to CHORISTER 1, in jest) Praise the Lord.

CHORISTER 2
Look, I said!

CHORISTER 3
What?

CHORISTER 1
Who that?

CHORISTER 3
Lord.

CHORISTER 2
Beulah Beatrice Brown.

CHORISTER 1
My lord.

CHORISTERS
So sad.

CHORISTER 2
How she come to die again?

CHORISTER 1
It was that rigoritis.

CHORISTERS 2 & 3
Huh?

CHORISTER 1
No. Low blood I think it was.

CHORISTER 3
Somethin' 'bout her heart?

CHORISTER 1
Yes. Cardiology.

CHORISTER 2
(to CHORISTER 3) Didn't she have gangrene?

CHORISTER 1
No. I remember now. It was asbestos.

CHORISTER 3 reacts.

CHORISTER 2
(to CHORISTER 3) Alzheimer's.

CHORISTERS 2 & 3 share a laugh.

CHORISTER 1
God rest ya, / BB.

CHORISTER 2
(still laughing) Amen.

CHORISTER 1
God / rest ya.

CHORISTERS 2 & 3
(still laughing) God rest your soul.

CHORISTER 3 sees SAMUEL at ANNA's gravesite.

CHORISTER 3
(to CHORISTER 2) Look.

The humming stops.

Anna.

CHORISTER 1 snickers.

CHORISTER 2
(to CHORISTER 1) Shhh!

JOHN SOLOMON
(singing) I'm gonna meet my mother in the wilderness
The wilderness, the wilderness
I'm gonna meet my mother in the wilderness
One of those days.

SAMUEL crosses to JOHN SOLOMON.

(singing) I'm going right straight up yonder
I'm going right straight up yonder
I'm going right straight up yonder
One of those days.

Scene 8

In 2010 JOHN SOLOMON is at home playing guitar. He sings, alternating between high and low octaves.

JOHN SOLOMON
(singing) I'm gonna sing and shout up in the wilderness

SAMUEL enters, unbeknownst to JOHN SOLOMON.

The wilderness, the wilderness
I'm gonna sing and shout up in the wilderness

SAMUEL joins in the singing.

JOHN SOLOMON & SAMUEL
One of those days.

Beat.

SAMUEL
That a new verse?

Beat.

Sound good.

JOHN SOLOMON
I'm tryna get a good balance of the high and the low.

SAMUEL
I like it.

JOHN SOLOMON
Sure you do.

Beat.

G'on. Take it.

JOHN SOLOMON hands the guitar to SAMUEL. GHOST ANNA is nearby, listening and enjoying the family time.

You can have that one. You know I got more where that come from.

SAMUEL
Don't I know it.

SAMUEL strums a tune on the guitar.

JOHN SOLOMON
What that?

SAMUEL
Workin' on a new song.

SAMUEL plays a short, fancy chord progression.

Can't quite get the chords I want though.

JOHN SOLOMON
Boy, how many times I got to tell you—all it take is two, three chords at the most.

SAMUEL gently mocks his father.

JOHN SOLOMON & SAMUEL
Three chords'll get you three hundred hymns if you know how to work 'em.

JOHN SOLOMON
Hmph! Sittin' over there actin' like you ain't got no home trainin'.

JOHN SOLOMON grabs guitar from SAMUEL.

Bougie-ass muh'fucka.

SAMUEL
Pops.

JOHN SOLOMON
(singing, playing) Jesus loves me this I know
For the Bible tell me so
Little ones to Him belong
They are weak but He is strong

Father and son sing together, backed by the ENSEMBLE.

JOHN SOLOMON & SAMUEL
Yes, Jesus loves me
Yes, Jesus loves me
Yes, Jesus loves me
For the Bible tells me so

JOHN SOLOMON
There, you see now?

JOHN SOLOMON strums three chords.

One, two, and . . .

He plays the wrong chord.

Shit! Wait . . . one, two, and . . . three! There it go!

JOHN SOLOMON strums an easy rhythm on one chord, slightly out of tune and with the wrong notes from time to time.

Pick a hymn. Any hymn.

SAMUEL
Pops.

JOHN SOLOMON
C'mon! Sing somethin'.

SAMUEL
Pops, we been through this how many times?

JOHN SOLOMON
And you still ain't learned it otherwise you woulda had that new song writ by now. C'mon.

JOHN SOLOMON continues strumming.

SAMUEL
(singing) Swing low, sweet chariot . . .

JOHN SOLOMON joins in the singing.

JOHN SOLOMON & SAMUEL
(singing) Comin' for to carry me home
Swing low, sweet chariot
Comin' for to carry me home

JOHN SOLOMON
See that? One, two, three. Keep singin'. C'mon.

SAMUEL
(singing) I looked over Jordan and what did I see

JOHN SOLOMON
(interrupting) Tell 'em what you see, boy!

JOHN SOLOMON & SAMUEL
(singing) Comin' for to carry me home

SAMUEL
(singing) A band of angels comin' after me

JOHN SOLOMON & SAMUEL
(singing) Comin' for to carry me home

JOHN SOLOMON
(interrupting) Swing it on low now now . . .

SAMUEL
(singing) Swing low . . .

JOHN SOLOMON & SAMUEL
(singing) . . . sweet chariot
Comin' for to carry me home
Swing low, sweet chariot
Comin' for to carry me home

JOHN SOLOMON continues strumming a single chord.

SAMUEL
Aight then, thanks, Pops, I'm good / to go now.

JOHN SOLOMON
(singing) I'm gonna lay down my burden

SAMUEL
I can't believe this.

JOHN SOLOMON
(singing) Down by the riverside
Down by the riverside
Down by the riverside
Said I'm gonna lay down my burden

SAMUEL
(singing) Down by the riverside

JOHN SOLOMON
(singing) I ain't gon' study to war no more

JOHN SOLOMON picks up the pace a bit.

JOHN SOLOMON & SAMUEL
(singing) I ain't gon' study to war no more, study to war no more
Study to war no more
I ain't gon' study to war no more, study to war no more
Study to war no more

SAMUEL
Okay then / I . . .

JOHN SOLOMON
(singing) I'm gonna lay down / my sword and shield

SAMUEL
Pops.

JOHN SOLOMON
(singing) Down by the riverside
Down by the riverside
Down by the riverside
Said I'm gonna lay down my sword and shield, way down

(speaking) C'mon, / Sammy!

SAMUEL
(singing) Down by the / riverside

JOHN SOLOMON
(singing) I ain't gon' study to war no more

SAMUEL
Okay, that's enough.

JOHN SOLOMON really picks up the pace.

JOHN SOLOMON
(singing) I ain't gon' study to war no more, study to war no more
I ain't gon' study to war no more
I ain't gon' study to war no more, study to war no more

(big finish) Study to war no mo-ore

SAMUEL
Aight, Pops, thanks, I'm good, now let me see the guitar I'll finish / writing that song.

JOHN SOLOMON
(singing, fervently) Said I'mma gonna put on my long white robe

SAMUEL
Pops!

JOHN SOLOMON
One more.

SAMUEL
It's never just one more with you.

JOHN SOLOMON
Just one.

SAMUEL
Last time I almost shit myself 'cause you ain't know when to / stop.

JOHN SOLOMON
C'mon, Sammy! Just one more hymn and I'll stop.

SAMUEL
(sarcastically) Right.

JOHN SOLOMON
My word on it. Pick somethin'. I got you. C'mon.

Beat.

C'mon!

SAMUEL dramatically clears his throat and begins singing in a booming operatic voice, off-time to the music.

SAMUEL
(singing, in jest) When Israel was in Egypt land
Let my people go

JOHN SOLOMON stops strumming.

Oppressed so hard / they could . . .

JOHN SOLOMON
(interrupting) What in the / shit . . .

SAMUEL
(interrupting, singing) Go down / Moses . . .

JOHN SOLOMON
What the shit is that?

JOHN SOLOMON plays chords as he calls their number—one, two, and three.

I said one, two, and three.

JOHN SOLOMON plays random, dissonant chords now—four, five, and six.

Think you smart comin' up here wit' four, five, and six.

SAMUEL
Pops!

JOHN SOLOMON
Sing the hymn like I tell ya!

SAMUEL
Aight then!

JOHN SOLOMON
Aight then! C'mon!

JOHN SOLOMON starts strumming again.

SAMUEL
(singing) There is a balm in Gilead

JOHN SOLOMON stops strumming.

To make the wounded whole

SAMUEL and GHOST ANNA sing together.

There is a balm in Gilead
To heal the sin-sick soul

GHOST ANNA
(singing) Sometimes I feel discouraged
And think my work's in vain

JOHN SOLOMON
Rocky come by today.

Beat.

Say he seen you talkin' to Eli after the funeral.

JOHN SOLOMON puts down his guitar and picks up a wooden cross; he carves. GHOST ANNA continues singing through the scene.

SAMUEL
We was just talkin' about Mama Irenie / is all.

JOHN SOLOMON
Bullshit. What he want.

JOHN SOLOMON stops carving.

Boy, don't make me ask you again.

SAMUEL
It was nothin', Pops. Really.

Beat.

He just . . . He asked if . . . He said I should come by the church sometime . . .

JOHN SOLOMON reacts.

. . . but only if I wanted to and I / didn't say I was . . .

JOHN SOLOMON
Why he want you to come?

Beat.

SAMUEL
Just to . . . to talk about Mama Irenie.

JOHN SOLOMON reacts.

He wants to talk about Mom.

JOHN SOLOMON resumes his wood carving.

JOHN SOLOMON
What about her?

SAMUEL
Just somethin' belongs to her; he wants me to have it.

JOHN SOLOMON
Bastard.

SAMUEL
Pops.

JOHN SOLOMON
Boy, how many times I have to tell you that man is the devil?

SAMUEL
Well I never said I would meet him / and besides . . .

JOHN SOLOMON
You shoulda told him no!

SAMUEL
He wants to talk about my mother! And since you never talk about her / I figured . . .

JOHN SOLOMON
I said no!

SAMUEL
He has her prayer cross! Said she left it up church one day and that he been tryin' to give it to you but you won't even talk to him!

JOHN SOLOMON
'Cause he's the devil!

SAMUEL
Are you listenin' to what I'm / sayin'?

JOHN SOLOMON
Boy, don't you dare talk to me like / I'm some kinda . . .

SAMUEL
He has my mother's prayer cross! The one she wore in every picture. The one she never took off. What else was I supposed to do? All these years you been keeping me from her . . .

JOHN SOLOMON gets up.

. . . keeping me from him, and for what? You think I don't know?

JOHN SOLOMON
What you / know?

SAMUEL
Think I never heard Cousin Paulina and 'em gossipin' / all while I was growin' up?

JOHN SOLOMON
So you gonna believe / Paulina and 'em?

SAMUEL
They *still* talkin'. They was talkin' today / up by the church!

JOHN SOLOMON
Over me? Your father?

SAMUEL
Are you my father?

GHOST ANNA stops singing.

I didn't mean that.

JOHN SOLOMON fumbles around the room.

I'm sorry. Pops, I didn't mean it. I know you're my father—all I'm sayin' is that sometimes I wish you would just talk to me. Talk to *him*. He's your brother. *And* a man of God, that's gotta count for somethin'?

Beat.

Pops!

JOHN SOLOMON
You want a prayer cross, do ya?

JOHN SOLOMON throws a wooden cross at SAMUEL.

GHOST ANNA
John.

JOHN SOLOMON grabs a box full of wooden crosses he's carved and throws them at SAMUEL. GHOST ANNA feels a sharp pain in her abdomen; she reaches for JOHN SOLOMON to help her, writhing in pain.

JOHN SOLOMON
And you can give them ones to the good reverend / 'cause he gonna need all the help he can get . . .

SAMUEL
I'm done. Done!

JOHN SOLOMON
. . . but you mark my words, Mister Samuel Jeremiah Ezekial Leviticus Moses . . .

SAMUEL
(interrupting) Same shit, different day.

JOHN SOLOMON
. . . you better hear what I'm sayin' to you, boy . . .

SAMUEL
(interrupting) Do you even hear what you're sayin' half the time?

JOHN SOLOMON
. . . 'cause ain't a prayer in the whole world can save that no-good-for-nothin' fake-ass lyin' preachin' motherfucker.

SAMUEL
(interrupting) And you wonder why I ain't been home in four years.

GHOST ANNA
(reaching for help) John.

JOHN SOLOMON
And ain't a prayer can save me neither.*

SAMUEL
(interrupting) I'm so over this shit.

JOHN SOLOMON
So you might as well take 'em.

> *JOHN SOLOMON is retrieving boxes of crosses he's stashed around the living room and throwing them at SAMUEL.*

SAMUEL
Twenty-two years, Pops.

JOHN SOLOMON
Take 'em all.

GHOST ANNA
John, please.

SAMUEL
In twenty-two years you've hardly said her name.

JOHN SOLOMON
Think you sumthin' now, do you? Come talk to *me* / like that?

GHOST ANNA
John.

---

* Pronounced "nee-ther."

SAMUEL
What happened?

JOHN SOLOMON
Tell me who I should and shouldn't be talkin' to?

SAMUEL
I got a right to know.

JOHN SOLOMON
You don't know shit!

He throws a whole box of crosses at SAMUEL.

That lyin' sonafabitch probably done slept with half the women in the community *includin'* your . . .

GHOST ANNA
(interrupting, frantic) John.

JOHN SOLOMON
And you come home. Home to bury Mama Irenie. Come home thinkin' you "all that" just 'cause you got the hell up outta this . . . this . . .

He throws another box of crosses at SAMUEL.

Mr. "Superstar" with your five, six, and seven and God know how many more chords you know more'n me, thinkin' you know somethin'—you don't know shit.

GHOST ANNA
John, please.

JOHN SOLOMON
You don't think I ever wanted to get the hell up outta here? Huh? I stayed here for you. All this this . . .

JOHN SOLOMON throws crosses.

JOHN SOLOMON
(to SAMUEL) . . . for you.

GHOST ANNA
(to JOHN SOLOMON) STOP!

SAMUEL hears GHOST ANNA. GHOST ANNA reaches for JOHN SOLOMON.

SAMUEL
(to JOHN SOLOMON, knowingly) Mom.

GHOST ANNA is on the floor, twisting with labour pains.

(looking up) Mom?

JOHN SOLOMON
Ain't no point to it.

Beat.

She dead.

The CHORISTERS sing a funeral wail. SAMUEL exits, unbeknownst to JOHN SOLOMON.

Act 3
Scene 1

The CHORISTERS *sing a funeral wail. In 2010* JOHN SOLOMON *is at home, liquor nearby. He is intoxicated and his speech is somewhat broken. Wooden crosses are scattered everywhere.*

JOHN SOLOMON
Listen, Sammy. The Bible say to train up a child in the way he should go, and when he gets old he won't stray from it. That's why I gave you five Christian names—thought it'd keep you holy. And sanctified. But how can the spirit of God live here, in this place?

Beat.

Sammy, listen when I tell you this. You can't ever sort out that bridge between heaven and earth till you reconcile that bridge in your own heart. 'Cause sometimes, the most disgustin' things can happen in the holiest places.

Beat.

And some folks think morals is separate from religion. And some folks think the world is separate from God. But you best not to believe 'em, Sammy.

Beat.

Sammy, you hear me? Don't let that robe fool you. A man of God, he just a man.

The CHORISTERS *stop singing.*

Sammy.

Beat.

Sammy!

JOHN SOLOMON *realizes* SAMUEL *has left the house and he is alone. He grabs his rifle and exits.*

Scene 2

In 2010 REVEREND ELI *is at church.* JOHN SOLOMON *enters, visibly holding the rifle.*

JOHN SOLOMON
Been a long time since I stepped foot up here.

REVEREND ELI *reacts.* JOHN SOLOMON *picks up a Bible from a church pew.*

REVEREND ELI
What do you want, John.

JOHN SOLOMON
I come to have church, Reverend.

JOHN SOLOMON tosses the Bible at REVEREND ELI.

Open it.

REVEREND ELI picks up the Bible.

Deuteronomy 22:22. Find it.

REVEREND ELI finds the passage.

Read.

Beat.

Out loud so I can hear you.

REVEREND ELI
(reading) "If a man is / found . . . "

JOHN SOLOMON
Louder.

REVEREND ELI
"If a man is found sleeping / with . . . "

JOHN SOLOMON aims the rifle at REVEREND ELI.

JOHN SOLOMON
Louder!

REVEREND ELI
"If a man is found sleeping with another man's wife, both the man who slept with her and the woman must die."

JOHN SOLOMON
Thus saith the Lord.

REVEREND ELI
Brother, / I . . .

JOHN SOLOMON
I am not your brother.

REVEREND ELI
Please, John.

Beat.

Mama's gone.

Beat.

You and Samuel's the only family I got and I know I ain't done right by you but . . .

JOHN SOLOMON threatens REVEREND ELI.

Okay okay okay I'm sorry.

JOHN SOLOMON
Sorry nothin'! You stay the fuck away from Sammy, you hear me?

Beat.

Just stay away from Sammy.

REVEREND ELI
John.

JOHN SOLOMON exits. The CHORISTERS and ENSEMBLE whisper/gossip.

Scene 3

The ENSEMBLE continues to whisper/gossip as the CHORISTERS move through the graveyard towards the bridge. CHORISTER 1 hums a free, improvised, solo rendition of the funeral wail.

CHORISTER 2
Marcus.

CHORISTER 3
Marcus Jeremiah Ross.

CHORISTER 2
Break and entering.

CHORISTER 3
Armed robbery.

CHORISTER 2
Assault with a deadly weapon.

CHORISTER 3
Bobby.

CHORISTER 2
Johnson.

CHORISTER 3
Robert David Johnson.

CHORISTER 2
Soo fat.

CHORISTER 3
Maggots.

CHORISTER 2
Feastin'. Forty. Fifty.

CHORISTER 3
Fifty years to come.

CHORISTER 2
Mary.

CHORISTER 3
Mary Elizabeth Carter.

CHORISTER 2
Forgot you was / even dead.

CHORISTER 3
I forgot you was dead.

CHORISTER 2 & 3
Sorry.

CHORISTER 3
Charles . . .

CHORISTER 2
Charles.

CHORISTER 3
. . . Richard Johnson.

CHORISTER 2
Six . . .

CHORISTER 3
Seven.

CHORISTER 2
. . . wives.

CHORISTER 3
Beulah . . .

CHORISTER 2
Beulah Beatrice Brown.

CHORISTER 3
. . . Beatrice Brown.

CHORISTER 2
Irenie.

CHORISTER 3
Irene Isabella Moses.

JOHN SOLOMON
"My God."

CHORISTERS 2 & 3
Anna.

JOHN SOLOMON
"My God."

CHORISTER 1 stops humming.

CHORISTERS
John.

The ENSEMBLE stops gossiping.

JOHN SOLOMON
"Why hast thou forsaken me?"

Scene 4

In 2010 JOHN SOLOMON *is on the bridge reciting scripture from memory, liquor flask in hand.*

JOHN SOLOMON
"Why art thou so far from helping me."

Beat.

"I cry to thee in the daytime, but thou hearest not; and in the night season, and am not silent."

Beat.

"Our fathers trusted in thee: they trusted! and thou didst deliver them. They cried unto thee and were delivered!"

Beat.

"But I am . . . "

CHORISTER 3
John Solomon Moses.

CHORISTER *1 hums a free, improvised, solo rendition of the funeral wail.*

JOHN SOLOMON
" . . . a worm."

CHORISTER 2
"A worm."

JOHN SOLOMON
"A no man;"

CHORISTER 3
"A no man;"

CHORISTER 2
"a reproach / of men!"

JOHN SOLOMON
"a reproach of men! And . . . "

JOHN SOLOMON & CHORISTERS 2 & 3
" . . . despised of the people."

The ENSEMBLE *whispers/gossips.*

JOHN SOLOMON
"All they that see me laugh me to scorn: they shoot out the lip, they shake the head, saying . . . "

JOHN SOLOMON & CHORISTER 3
" . . . He trusted on the LORD that He would deliver him: (so) let *Him* deliver him, seeing he delighted in Him."

GHOST ANNA appears.

JOHN SOLOMON
"Have mercy on me, O God . . . "

Beat.

" . . . according to your unfailing love; according to your great compassion. Blot out my transgressions."

JOHN SOLOMON douses himself with alcohol.

"Wash away all my iniquity. And cleanse me from my . . . "

JOHN SOLOMON moves forward as if to jump off the bridge; the ENSEMBLE stops whispering; CHORISTERS 2 & 3 react; CHORISTER 1 keeps humming the funeral wail; GHOST ANNA reaches for JOHN SOLOMON, touches him—he reacts.

"Be not far from me for trouble is near. For there is none to help."

JOHN SOLOMON exits hurriedly.

Scene 5

In 2010 SAMUEL enters the church.

SAMUEL
Hello?

CHORISTER 1 stops humming.

Hello?

Beat.

Uncle Eli?

REVEREND ELI
Samuel?

Beat.

REVEREND ELI
Did you just call me . . .

SAMUEL
I just came by to . . .

Beat.

REVEREND ELI
(suddenly anxious) Does John know you're here?

SAMUEL
No.

REVEREND ELI
Are you sure?

SAMUEL
I'm sure.

Beat.

REVEREND ELI
You're early for Bible study.

SAMUEL
You said I should come see you. About my mother's prayer cross.

REVEREND ELI
Right, right . . . of course, it's right here.

REVEREND ELI retrieves the prayer cross; he pauses with it for a moment before handing it to SAMUEL.

SAMUEL
How did you know my mother?

Beat.

I mean, do you remember her?

YOUNG ANNA appears.

REVEREND ELI
Of course. I remember.

SAMUEL
What do you remember?

REVEREND ELI
She was beautiful. And kind.

REVEREND ELI crosses to YOUNG ANNA.

Warm. She was, truly, an angel.

In 1988 JOHN SOLOMON looks on from behind.

She looked like heaven. And she felt like home.

Lights fade on YOUNG ANNA and JOHN SOLOMON, leaving REVEREND ELI alone and facing the darkness. The CHORISTERS sing the funeral wail.

SAMUEL
How did she die?

YOUNG ANNA groans.

REVEREND ELI
Well . . . you know she had breast cancer.

YOUNG ANNA
John. It's time.

REVEREND ELI
And she had to have a operation.

YOUNG ANNA
John, I don't feel too . . .

YOUNG ANNA crosses to JOHN SOLOMON; he avoids her.

SAMUEL
Yeah but that didn't kill her.

YOUNG ANNA
John.

JOHN SOLOMON bars the door so YOUNG ANNA can't leave.

What are you doing?

REVEREND ELI
No.

YOUNG ANNA
John.

YOUNG ANNA moves to leave; JOHN SOLOMON blocks the door.

John, let me out.

SAMUEL
It was me, wasn't it.

The CHORISTERS' *singing intensifies.*

REVEREND ELI
What?

JOHN SOLOMON *and* YOUNG ANNA *continue to struggle.*

SAMUEL
She died because of me.

REVEREND ELI
How can you even think that you had anything to do with it?

SAMUEL
I know she died the same year I was born.

YOUNG ANNA
John, please.

YOUNG ANNA *groans.*

SAMUEL
Don't gotta be a genius to figure out what happened.

JOHN SOLOMON *exits through the front door;* YOUNG ANNA *sees him, groans.*

REVEREND ELI
Samuel.

SAMUEL
(interrupting) I killed her.

YOUNG ANNA
John.

YOUNG ANNA trips, hits her head on the wood stove, falls to the floor, lays motionless.

SAMUEL
I killed my mother.

REVEREND ELI
(to SAMUEL) No.

JOHN SOLOMON
(to YOUNG ANNA) No.

REVEREND ELI looks over to YOUNG ANNA.

REVEREND ELI
It wasn't like that. It was an accident.
She waited too long to get to the hospital.
It wasn't your fault.

JOHN SOLOMON rushes to YOUNG ANNA. He shakes her. He checks her eyes and listens to see if she's breathing before realizing that she is dead.

SAMUEL
Did she suffer?

Beat.

Did she?

REVEREND ELI
Huh? No.

Beat.

No, son, she didn't. She was gone before you were even born.
Complications with the pregnancy.

JOHN SOLOMON plots to save baby SAMUEL—he retrieves a sharp knife and a bottle of alcohol; he sterilizes the knife with alcohol and makes an incision; he cuts baby SAMUEL from YOUNG ANNA's womb. The baby cries; JOHN SOLOMON reacts.

Samuel, listen to me. This is not your fault. You are a miracle. You hear me? You are a blessing from God.

SAMUEL
The same God that took my mother? The same God that gave me a father who blames me?

REVEREND ELI
John doesn't blame you for this.

SAMUEL
Yes he does.

JOHN SOLOMON washes baby SAMUEL with a cloth.

That's why he won't ever talk about it. Why he treats me like one of them crosses he sits carvin' day in and day out like . . . like I'm somethin' he can shape and mould and make holy.

REVEREND ELI
Samuel.

SAMUEL
Like God don't see him all day cussin' and drinkin'.

The CHORISTERS stop humming.

REVEREND ELI
Samuel, John loves you.

JOHN SOLOMON wraps baby SAMUEL in a towel.

He may not be the best at showin' it but you gotta know that he loves you. More than you could ever know.

Beat.

Come. Pray with me.

SAMUEL shakes his head no.

Come on. Let's pray.

SAMUEL
You know how to do it better than me. I never went to church.

REVEREND ELI
All you have to do is open your heart. Talk to God.

Beat.

SAMUEL
There's this one prayer Pops taught me. We used to say it sometimes. It's from the Bible.

REVEREND ELI bows his head; SAMUEL does too.

"Have mercy on me, O God . . . "

CHORISTER 3 hums one round of the doxology "Praise God from Whom All Blessings Flow," or the "Old 100th."

" . . . according to your unfailing love; according to your great compassion. Blot out my transgressions. Wash away all my iniquity, and . . . "

JOHN SOLOMON joins SAMUEL's prayer—he is holding Baby SAMUEL. He washes the baby with a wet cloth.

SAMUEL & JOHN SOLOMON
" . . . cleanse me from my sin. Surely I was sinful at birth, sinful from the time my mother conceived me."

JOHN SOLOMON squeezes water from the washcloth; he washes baby SAMUEL.

"Cleanse me with hyssop, and I will be clean; wash me, and I will be whiter than snow."

JOHN SOLOMON continues the prayer alone.

JOHN SOLOMON
"Create in me a pure heart, O God, and renew a steadfast spirit within me. Save me from bloodguilt, O God, and my tongue will sing of your righteousness. O Lord, open my lips, and my mouth will declare your praise."

The humming stops. JOHN SOLOMON speaks to baby SAMUEL.

We gon' sing, boy.

Beat.

I'm gon' teach you to sing. Just like y'mama.
(singing) There is a balm in Gilead

SAMUEL joins in the singing, father and son sing together, from separate scenes.

JOHN SOLOMON & SAMUEL
(singing) To make the . . .

JOHN SOLOMON hears SAMUEL singing; he reacts.

SAMUEL
(singing) . . . wounded whole.

JOHN SOLOMON hears SAMUEL. He leaves baby SAMUEL and moves towards the church.

There is a balm in Gilead
To heal the sin-sick soul

JOHN SOLOMON sees SAMUEL and REVEREND ELI together in church; GHOST ANNA reaches out to JOHN SOLOMON, an invitation for reconciliation.

Sometimes I feel discouraged . . .

JOHN SOLOMON exits hurriedly; GHOST ANNA calls after him.

GHOST ANNA
John.

SAMUEL
(singing) . . . And think my work's in vain
But then the Holy Spirit
Revives my soul again
Revives my soul again

Scene 6

In 2010 JOHN SOLOMON *arrives home to find* YOUNG ANNA*'s shawl draped across his chair. The family Bible and portrait are also out in plain sight.* JOHN SOLOMON *puts the rifle on the table next to the Bible. He picks up* YOUNG ANNA*'s shawl; he mourns her death.* REVEREND ELI *and* SAMUEL *speak from the church.*

REVEREND ELI
You're a good boy, Samuel. My brother raised you well.

JOHN SOLOMON *sees* SAMUEL *and* REVEREND ELI.

SAMUEL
You should tell him that.

REVEREND ELI
I will.

Beat.

I will.

GHOST ANNA *sings to* JOHN SOLOMON, *almost a whisper.*

GHOST ANNA
(whispering, singing) There is a balm in Gilead
To make the wounded whole
There is a balm in Gilead
To heal the sin-sick soul

JOHN SOLOMON *takes the rifle and puts it to his temple, threatening to pull the trigger. The* CHORISTERS *look on.*

Sometimes I feel discouraged
And think my work's in vain
But then the Holy Spirit
Revives my soul again
Revives my soul again

As the next verse is sung, JOHN SOLOMON *collects the Bible and photo. He wraps them inside* YOUNG ANNA*'s shawl. The* CHORISTERS *sing along from the shadows.*

CHORISTERS & GHOST ANNA
(singing) There is a balm in Gilead
To make the wounded whole
There is a balm in Gilead
To heal the sin-sick soul

JOHN SOLOMON *crosses the bridge, moving towards the church.*

Sometimes I feel discouraged
And think my work's in vain
But then the Holy Spirit

JOHN SOLOMON *enters the church carrying* YOUNG ANNA*'s items.* REVEREND ELI *moves to greet his brother.*

Revives my soul again
Revives my soul again

End.

Shauntay Grant is a Canadian playwright, poet, performance artist, and children's author. She is an associate professor of creative writing at Dalhousie University, a member of the College of the Royal Society of Canada, and former poet laureate for the City of Halifax. Her work examines African Nova Scotian and African diasporic history and culture, as well as contemporary approaches to literature and performance. Grant's work has been commissioned by Against the Grain Theatre, Boca del Lupo, Eastern Front Theatre, and Obsidian Theatre Company. Her other honours include a Joseph S. Stauffer Prize from the Canada Council for the Arts, a Robert Merritt Award from Theatre Nova Scotia, a Best Atlantic-Published Book Award from the Atlantic Book Awards, a Poet of Honour prize from the Canadian Festival of Spoken Word, and a Marilyn Baillie Picture Book Award from the Canadian Children's Book Centre for *Africville* (Groundwood Books).

First edition: April 2021
Printed and bound in Canada by Rapido Books, Montreal

Jacket painting by Natia Lemay
Author photo © Shyronn Smardon

PLAYWRIGHTS
CANADA PRESS
202-269 Richmond St. W.
Toronto, ON
M5V 1X1

416.703.0013
info@playwrightscanada.com
www.playwrightscanada.com
@playcanpress